BODMIN M

Through the Years

E.V. Thompson

BOSSINEY BOOKS

First published in 1992 by Bossiney Books,
St Teath, Bodmin, Cornwall.

Typeset and printed by
Penwell Print Ltd, Callington, Cornwall.

ISBN 0 948158 81 6

ACKNOWLEDGEMENTS

Front cover design: MAGGIE GINGER
Front cover photograph: RAY BISHOP
Back cover: RAY BISHOP
Other photographs: JOHN LYNE , CLIFFORD CLEMENS
Drawings: FELICITY YOUNG

*The author would like to thank the
staff of the Cornish Studies Library for their
help and Sue Webb of Clemens Photography
for her father's photographs.*

*Front cover: Dozmary Pool.
Back cover: Distant views of Rough Tor and Brown Willy.*

ST BREWARD CHURCH PORCH

Most churches are cloaked in an air of timelessness. St Breward's parish church is no exception. Even the gravestones seem to be communing as once did the villagers whose life they commemorate.

ABOUT THE AUTHOR AND THE BOOK

E.V. THOMPSON, acknowledged as one of the West Country's most successful international authors, has lived in Cornwall for twenty-two years, by far the longest period he has spent in one place during his lifetime.

Born in London, he was taken to Oxfordshire as a small boy, when the family lost its home during the World War II blitz. He left Burford Grammar School at the age of fifteen to spend nine years in the Royal Navy.

Unable to settle down to civilian life after his Navy years, E.V. Thompson joined the Bristol Police Force and was a founder member of that city's Vice Squad. After six years he left the police to work as an investigator with B.O.A.C. (now British Airways). During this time he worked with the Hong Kong Police Narcotics Bureau and was later appointed Chief Security Officer of Rhodesia's Department of Civil Aviation.

After having some two hundred short stories published and broadcast, E.V. Thompson returned to England determined to become a full-time writer. A year later, broke but still writing, he swept factory floors in a clay works at Par, home of a small South Cornish industrial port.

In 1976 his book, Chase the Wind *won a 'Best Historical Novel' competition and became a bestseller. This novel, the story of a 19th century copper mining community on the beautiful but harsh Bodmin Moor has been followed by sixteen more novels. Many of these are set in Cornwall, others take the reader to Africa, America, Scotland, Ireland, Australia and Canada.*

E.V. Thompson now lives in a charming house overlooking the sea, not far from Mevagissey, with his wife, two school-age sons and a wide variety of pets.

He frequently returns to Bodmin Moor and freely admits that this wild, lonely and unspoiled area has a magic that has inspired many of his books and served as an occasional tonic to combat the demands of life as a best-selling author.

In Bodmin Moor Through The Ages, *the author's sixth work for Bossiney, he has gathered another collection of photographs representing life on Bodmin Moor from the early years of the century until the present day. Some, like the photograph of London evacuees stroking sheep, animals they will never have seen before arriving in Cornwall, strike a chord with the author. On his arrival in an Oxfordshire village, shocked and shaken from a terrifying night of exploding bombs, he shared space at the hearth of a country cottage with a new-born litter of piglets!*

This is a book for lovers of Old Cornwall and those who know and enjoy Bodmin Moor. It is also a book for those who have yet to discover this ancient, timeless heart of Cornwall.

E.V. THOMPSON
   The author, as portrayed by painter Nicholas St John
Rosse of Trethevy, Tintagel.

INTRODUCING BODMIN MOOR THROUGH THE YEARS

RISING AT the very heart of Cornwall is an expanse of land that, in cold, geological language, is recorded as a granite moorland, granite being defined as an igneous rock of a crystalline nature.

No doubt such a description is accurate, as far as it goes. This is certainly moorland, and granite is to be seen everywhere. Granite ridges dominate the hill-tops, lop-sided granite peaks soar over farmhouse and marsh and granite boulders push through the coarse moorland grass with the profusion of mushrooms in a meadow.

Yet it is impossible accurately to describe this upland gem using the language of one of the sciences.

Bodmin Moor is small in area, with a radius of little more than ten miles in any direction. It is high land with tors and ridges, yet the highest point, Brown Willy, is only some four hundred and twenty metres above sea level.

But statistics cannot convey the mystique of Bodmin Moor. The sense of timelessness in a landscape that man has used in a variety of ways for tens of centuries, only to have the moor re-assert its claim of ownership, in its own good time.

Words, no matter how descriptive, cannot bring to life the feel of the wind assaulting ear drums. Days when grey clouds, low enough to touch, embrace the moor in a love affair that began the day the world was made.

Bodmin Moor has seen man advance from a primitive being who shaped his stone implements around the shores of Dozmary Pool. Through the ages those who lived and worked here have erected stone circles and built longhouses. Countless generations of tinners and copper miners have spread across the moor, tunnelling deep in the ground, using increasingly sophisticated means to extract ore. Ore that would enrich a fortunate few, and bring many, many more to a premature grave.

The monotonous, ground-shaking thud of ore-crushing stamps has long-gone and the old mine buildings are tumbling ruins, windowless and open-roofed. The alien sound most likely to be heard here today is the sudden startling roar of a jet engine as a Royal Air Force pilot practises low-flying in a multi-million pound warplane.

TEMPLE
A solitary windswept tree emphasises the starkness of the moorland.

continued on page 10

ST LUKE'S CHAPEL, near Bolventor.

In the days before the late Dame Daphne du Maurier's books turned Jamaica Inn into a tourist attraction, it was a dark and brooding moorland inn. Yet, many years before, John Wesley had passed this way, lighting a candle to his faith in the darkest corners of Bodmin Moor. Generations of moorland farmers and miners were born, married and died within the strictures of the Methodist church. Lonely St Luke's chapel was erected in the valley of the infant Fowey river in 1891, as a living monument to those who still worshipped as Wesley had dictated.

Many years before, another chapel, also dedicated to St Luke stood between Bolventor and Dozmary pool. For some two centuries men, women and children would troop from the remotest corners of the moor to worship in one or other of these chapels.

One of the most famous Methodist preachers was Isaac Foot. Member of Parliament for the area, he would ride to St Luke's from St Cleer, enjoying a view along the way that is little changed today.

BROWN WILLY, SEEN FROM ROUGHTOR

In this delightfully composed drawing by Felicity Young, she has captured both the ruggedness and the space of the moor. These are the two highest hills in Cornwall. Brown Willy is the higher at 1,375 feet. It is a comparatively modest height, but rising from the landscape of the moor it assumes the majesty and stature of a mountain.

But such sounds disturb the moor for seconds only. The visitor here is more likely to stop for the melody of a skylark or the echo of a lapwing's cry. Ever present too is the plaintive, far-reaching cry of a gliding buzzard, interrupted by the deeper, raucous call of a raven.

When I lived in a cottage on Bodmin Moor I always looked upon it as a magical place. I still do. Yet magic needs to be shared.

In the pages of this book are men, women and children who have lived or worked on or about Bodmin Moor. They will have shared in the magic and know that what I say is true.

I hope all those who read this book and who have not already done so, will visit Cornwall's moor and discover some of its magic for themselves.

E.V. THOMPSON

KINGS HEAD HOTEL, FIVE LANES

Built beside the old main London to Cornwall road in 1623, as a coaching inn, it was occupied by both Roundhead and Cavalier during the Civil War that raged through Cornwall a few years later.

Throughout its long history the inn has been known by many names. A hundred and fifty years after it was built it was known as the Indian Queen, later it became the London Inn and towards the end of the 18th century the Five Lanes Inn.

The King's Head is reputed to have its own ghost, a young lady who hanged herself here after her man left her to follow John Wesley.

CHAPEL OUTING AT DOZMARY POOL

This brooding expanse of water is where Excalibur, the sword of the legendary King Arthur, is reputed to have been committed to the water prior to the death of the warrior-king.

The pool was for very many years a favourite venue for chapel outings. Here, on a sunny summer's day, such an outing is being enjoyed by the members of St Luke's Methodist Church.

In this 1953 photograph there is more formality than would be seen on a similar occasion today.

BODMIN MOOR, near TEMPLE
  Moorland solitude can be found by merely turning one's
back on the busy A30 nearby. Temple has always been a
lonely and secret place. In the 18th century the entire male
population – two people – were hung for sheep-stealing.
  Once a settlement of the Knights Templar, the church
remained outside the jurisdiction of the Bishop until 1774
and was Cornwall's 'Gretna Green'.

▶

LAUNCESTON'S famous South Arch, or the Old South
Gateway.
Dominated by its castle, Launceston was known from
Norman times as 'Dunheved', or 'The city on a hill'. For
centuries it proudly wore the mantle of Cornwall's capital. The
rooms above the South Gate were once the town's gaol, the
second floor being for debtors.
Much more formidable were the dungeons of Launceston
Castle. Here the Quaker leader, George Fox, was imprisoned
in 1656, incarcerated for his faith and visited by the curious
and the sympathetic.

MOORLAND TRAVEL

Here the author and son Luke (head and feet just visible from his perch behind the seat) are driven along the beautiful Fowey river road, between Bolventor and Redgate, by Master Saddler Jane Talbot-Smith.

Jane's workshop, Blisland Harness Makers, is on this road and in addition to saddlery and leather work she is also able to build horse drawn vehicles.

The vehicle in the picture is drawn here by her horse Chateau Potensac. The dog – a Dalmatian – is a breed that was originally used as a carriage dog. Enjoying the exotic name Raki Plavina, Raki for short, it is another of Jane's pets.

DE LANK QUARRIES

Taken in 1945, this photograph shows an old man splitting granite, something that requires considerable skill and experience. Men such as this would know stone as a carpenter knows wood, working with its 'grain' and able to tell a good piece of stone from a bad one.

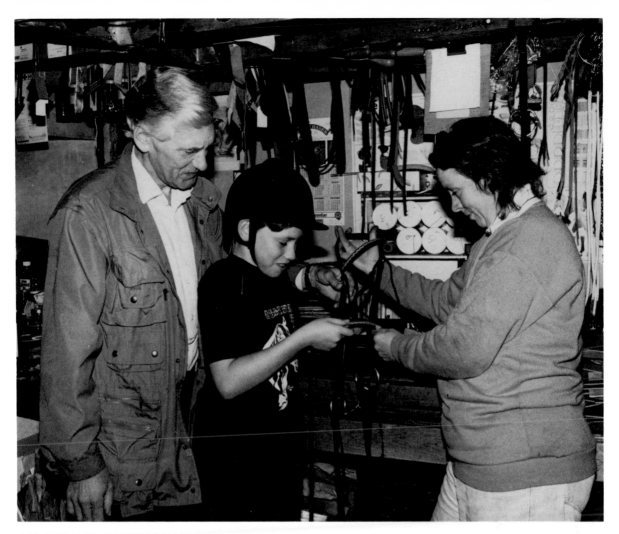

MOORLAND CRAFT

In this photograph, Jane Talbot-Smith presents the author's son, Luke, with the present especially made for his twelfth birthday, a superb bridle, while dad looks on.

Jane learned her craft initially at Cordwainers College, Hackney, an area of London well-known to the author in his childhood. She later worked for Master Saddler Les Coker, who made the side-saddle used regularly by HRH Queen Elizabeth II.

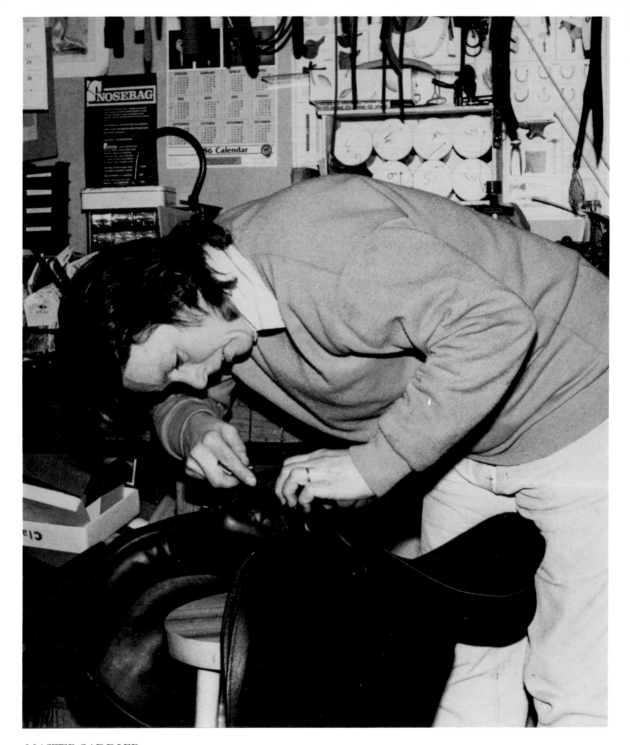

MASTER SADDLER

Bodmin Moor has always attracted talented men and women skilled in a remarkable variety of crafts.

Jane Talbot-Smith is seen here working on one of the beautiful saddles produced by her in her workshop, which is a glorious Aladdin's cave of leather and leatherwork of every description.

WENFORD BRIDGE

Potter Michael Cardew shows off his skills to African chiefs and overseas students at his Wenford Bridge pottery, on the edge of Bodmin Moor. He is using a technique that knows no frontiers. Potteries in Africa, the Middle East and Arabia use a similar method for throwing pots, even though the finished articles may have very differing shapes.

Liskeard, St. Cleer Village.

ST. CLEER.

ST CLEER in a quieter age

Situated just off the Eastern fringe of Bodmin Moor, St Cleer was at the heart of the copper mining community in the 19th century and it has absorbed much of the magical quality of the moor.

Some seven hundred and fifty feet above sea level, the village has a charming 'Holy Well' and an ancient cross. Not far away are Trethevy Quoit and Doniert's stone, a memorial to the Cornish 'King', who was drowned in the nearby river Fowey in AD 872.

WARTIME WHEELS

A white cycle for the dark days (and nights) of wartime Bodmin Moor. This photograph of Doreen Philp of St Cleer was taken on September 25, 1939. The second World War was only days old but the blackout was strictly enforced. With no street lighting and motor car headlights reduced to mere slits of light, Doreen Philps' father painted her bicycle white, so she might be seen more easily when cycling home from her work with Liskeard council.

War brought disruption even here in the remoteness of Bodmin Moor. Airfields were cut from its turf, aircraft crash-landed and allied soldiers speaking many languages trod its spongy turf.

COLLIFORD LAKE
Two views of this 20th century lake, formed to meet the needs of Cornwall's residents and the tens of thousands of summer visitors. There was great concern among naturalists and moorland lovers when the dam and lake were first proposed. There are some who still feel such a project is out of place here, but there are many others who believe the lake has added a new dimension to an area where each age of man has left something for posterity.

BLISLAND
A delightful farming photograph, taken on February 25 1950: triplet calves with their mother at F.C. Parnell's house.

ALTARNUN

These two old picture postcards show some of the marvellous carvings to be found in the church at Altarnun (spelled 'Altarnon' here). Known as the Cathedral of the Moor, this wonderful old church was fortunate to escape the sometimes insensitive 'improvements' of 19th century church restorers. The font is 12th century, while the magnificent pew ends date from 1510-1530.

Altarnon Church. South Aisle. | N.B. Bench Ends 1530.

ALTARNUN CHURCH

The 'Cathedral of the Moor'. At the very heart of Bodmin Moor, this beautiful old church has been by-passed by time and modern highways. The tall tower took more than a generation to construct and still dominates this moorland village despite severe storm damage in 1791, and again in 1810.

◀

ALTARNUN
This village is at the very heart of Bodmin Moor. Seen here working on a pair of cottages in 1910, is Samuel John Pooley (on the left), and some of his friends. The cottages would have been constructed of moorland granite with the addition of a few bricks, probably locally made.

CARDINHAM
Another of the moorland fringe villages. This scene depicts a way of life remembered by only a dwindling generation of moorland dwellers. For this man and his three strong, patient horses in the summer of 1942, 'intensive farming' was a phrase that had not yet been invented. The only threat to this traditional way of life was believed to be Adolf Hitler.

◀ *THE INDUSTRIAL HEART*
Men working at Hantergantick Quarry in April 1962.

KING DONIERT'S STONE

Now in two halves, this memorial stone is a monument to a little-known Cornish 'king' who was drowned in the nearby River Fowey. The weather worn inscription reads 'Doniert Rogavit pro Anima.' It tells the world at large that the memorial was raised 'For the good of Doniert's soul' in the 9th century, at a time when Cornwall was ruled from within its own borders.

Standing beside the road from Redgate to Minions, the memorial commemorates not only a forgotten leader, but a period of Cornish history that remains shrouded in legend, lore and mystery.

HELLAND VILLAGE

In January, 1947 the war between men of opposing nations was over, but moorland dwellers have waged a never-ending war with the elements from time immemorial.

In this photograph the County Council Roads Department is attempting to clear the roads of snow, using a primitive snow plough.

On the open moor conditions would be even more severe and farmers spend days battling through deep snow drifts in search of their sheep.

MOORLAND EDGE

In this photograph sheep are grazing on the edge of Bodmin Moor, close to both Helland and Tredethy. Although only relatively small, Bodmin is a moor of ever-changing character. In some places the change between farmland and moorland is sudden and stark. In other places, and the photograph shows one of them, the change is so gradual that it comes as a surprise to realise one or other has been left behind.

KILMAR TOR

This ragged and very impressive granite ridge lies close to my own favourite moorland peak, Sharptor. For many years around the turn of the century this area provided stone for the mine buildings and structures dotting the landscape hereabouts.

JAMAICA INN, BOLVENTOR

Immortalised by the late Dame Daphne du Maurier in the book bearing its name, Jamaica Inn is now more than four centuries old, having been built in 1547.

This ancient inn has had a chequered history, but it would always have been a welcome sight for travellers crossing the moor.

The inn is said to be haunted by a man who was murdered after drinking here. It also boasts a somewhat cantankerous parrot. After many years of answering to the name of Percy, the parrot recently confounded everyone by laying a number of eggs!

The inn also contains a room containing memorabilia of the author whose fictional characters have given their names to the inn's many bars.

THE LOUNGE, JAMAICA INN, BOLVENTOR.

INN SIGN, JAMAICA INN

Surely the best-known inn sign in the world. Visitors come from all over the world to see the inn, immortalised in Daphne du Maurier's novel of the same name. Many visitors are eager to be photographed standing beneath the inn sign and the end result must adorn family photograph albums in every country of the world.

Since the construction of a dual carriageway across this section of the moor, the Jamaica Inn has recaptured some of the atmosphere of quieter days. The inn has had a chequered past, being both a temperance house and a posting house in the last century.

JAMAICA INN, DAME DAPHNE DU MAURIER ROOM

The international fame of the Jamaica Inn stems from the writing of the late Dame Daphne du Maurier. In her book Jamaica Inn, *she has captured the brooding atmosphere of this moorland inn. It is fitting that the inn should honour her with a room containing some of the memorabilia from her home, Kilmarth. It was here she wrote* The House on the Strand.

JAMAICA INN

   Wine tasting at Jamaica Inn in 1960. Such an occasion would have been an unusual occasion 30 years ago when appreciably less wine was drunk in Cornwall. In many Cornish inns at the time it was quite impossible to buy a glass of wine.

BOLVENTOR CHURCH

Once the Sunday place of worship for many moorland dwellers, and the scene of joyous weddings, proud christenings and sad – often tragic – funerals.

Close to the popular Jamaica Inn, this now forlorn church is boarded up beside the A30 dual carriageway which bisects Bodmin Moor. The headstones in this lonely churchyard carry the names of families once well-known and respected on the moor. Many have moved away, unable to compete with the progress that has contributed to the demise of this church built by the Rodd family of Trebartha, in North Hill parish.

MOORLAND DELIGHT
One of the finest ways to view the moor is from the back of a
horse. Dame Daphne du Maurier enjoyed riding here as a
young woman. John Wesley, founder of the Methodist Church
lost his way here whilst riding across the moor in a
snowstorm.
In this photograph, riders from the Tall Trees Riding Stable
at Davidstow enjoy a ride beneath the heights of Rough Tor.

BOLVENTOR CHURCH
The simple but impressive interior of the moorland church,
depicted on a sepia postcard.

CARADON HILL

With a ruined engine house standing sentinel at its foot the hill, now adorned with a huge radio and television mast visible for very many miles, has witnessed thousands of years of moorland history. It overlooks the enigmatic 'Hurlers', the Bronze Age stone circles, which legend has it are men and women, turned to stone for 'Hurling' (an ancient Cornish game), on the Sabbath.

Not far away is the Longstone, a tall granite pillar engraved with a Celtic cross, one of many scattered on and around the moor.

On this hill in August, 1644, King Charles mustered his troops before they set off to score a notable victory against the Parliamentary troops.

In 1837, copper was discovered here, sparking off a mining boom that would make the lucky few rich and lead hundreds more to a premature grave.

More recently, a low flying jet aircraft sliced off one of the stays supporting the great mast and, although seriously injured in the ensuing crash, the pilot lived.

BRADFORD BRIDGE

Constructed of slabs of granite and bridging the River Delank, this is a traditional moorland bridge, of a type that has been built across moorland rivers since the earliest days. This alone is enough to give a timeless quality to any photograph and the dress of the two children tells us they belong to an earlier generation.

NORTH HILL

This is one of the least-photographed of all the villages fringing Bodmin Moor. Perhaps this explains why the village has retained a great deal of its charm.

In the church is a magnificent memorial to the Spoure family, residents of nearby Trebartha Hall, once described as the most magnificent family seat in the county. There were various houses built on the site of Trebartha Hall, but the last one was demolished soon after World War II.

CHEESEWRING QUARRY, BODMIN MOOR

The Cheesewring Quarry on Stowe's Hill was still working when this postcard was produced earlier this century. With a mineral railway linking the quarry to the port of Looe, moorland granite was shipped to the world.

The railway has long since gone and so too has the need for granite. Today the steep quarry walls are the haunt of ravens and a challenge for those who find a fascination in climbing sheer cliff faces.

Cheese Wring Quarry, near Liskeard

CHEESEWRING VILLAGE

The Cheesewring village of this early postcard is, of course, the present-day village of Minions. The public house, The Cheesewring, boasts of being sited higher than any other in Cornwall.

Nearby are the Hurlers and the famous rock formation from which the inn and the village of the postcard gain their name.

Once at the heart of the 19th century copper mining boom, this has been a populated area for thousands of years. The famous Rillaton Cup, a small, gold vessel dating from the early Bronze Age was discovered here in an ancient grave. Given as a gift to William IV, the genial 'Sailor King', rumour has it that this priceless national heirloom was used as a shaving mug in the royal bathroom. Now in the British Museum, a copy of the cup may be seen in the museum of the Royal Cornwall Institution, in Truro.

Cheese Wring Village, near Liskeard

BRADFORD
A moorland hamlet where the River Delank runs beneath a
traditional clapper bridge. Many lovers of Bodmin Moor
consider this to be the prettiest spot of all and visitors return
year after year.

THE HURLERS

One of the best known and most-photographed features of Bodmin Moor, the Hurlers typify the mystery and antiquity of this beautiful, windswept area. There are many theories about the origins of these stone circles, quite apart from the legendary explanations. One I favour, not so much for its possible accuracy, but for the picture it conjures up is that this was once the meeting place of all the region's chieftains, or 'kings'. Each tribe, or family group, was represented by a stone before which the chieftain would take his place on the day of a meeting.

In the place of a chieftain in our photograph is Kay Isbell, from nearby St Cleer.

OLD TIMER

Bodmin Moor is well-known for extremes of weather, experienced nowhere else in Cornwall. In spite of this, many of the moorland residents live long and busy lives. Thomas Philp of Pennant Farm, Blisland, was born in 1862. he is seen here, shocking corn, at the age of 94!

BODMIN ASSIZE COURT ▲

Padlocked and slumbering now, yet the sight of this greystone building has struck terror into the hearts of countless felons as they faced the gallows or transportation for their crimes. Many famous trials have taken place here, including that of the sad cripple, Matthew Weeks, hung in August 1844, for the murder of his flirtatious sweetheart, Charlotte Dymond at Rough Tor, on Bodmin Moor.

CARMINOW CROSS, NEAR BODMIN

(Not "Carminnon" Cross, as on this 1922 postcard). There can be few parishes in Cornwall which do not have their own granite cross, or fragment of one, dating back to the Dark Ages. They have been variously described as guiding travellers to a Christian community, or marking crossroads or the boundary o a Christian parish. The design of each cross depended upon the skill and inclination of the individual stone mason, working with primitive tools. This particular cross has been moved from its original site, due to road improvements and may now be seen by the traveller arriving at the roundabout outside Bodmin from the direction of the Glynn Valley.

◀

JUDGE'S PROCESSION, BODMIN

This photograph, taken almost fifty years ago, depicts a piece of Bodmin's history that is no more. Here, the procession of Mr Justice Tucker crosses the church square during the Assizes of 1945.

Bodmin, Carminnon Cross

When he was not riding the moors and preaching at lonely chapels, Isaac Foot greatly enjoyed reading. He admitted that books were his great love. He had been known to buy a whole library in order to obtain just one book.
Explaining his feelings for a book, he once said: 'I want it for my very own. I want it for the second reading, perhaps the third, or the fourth. I want it with my name in it, with my own mark and symbols and underlinings and references.'

ISAAC FOOT, MP
Father of the most celebrated family in the West Country, Isaac Foot was the archetypal crusader. Radical Liberal, staunch Methodist and eloquent orator in the cause of the law, Methodism, or politics, Foot was a self-taught man of immense personality.

ST BREWARD
   The laying of the
foundation stone at St
Breward Sunday School on
June 29 1957. The
ceremony was performed
by the Rt Hon Isaac Foot.

JOHN WESLEY'S COTTAGE, TREWINT

Since the construction of a by-pass, this small, moorland hamlet is once more a peaceful place, little changed since Wesley first arrived here in 1744.

A year before Wesley's arrival, the owners of the cottage, Digory and Elizabeth Isbell, had been converted to Methodism by two itinerant preachers. As a result they built a tiny two-room extension on the end of their small cottage to house the far-travelling evangelists.

In all, Wesley made six visits to Trewint and the cottage is now a museum depicting those early days. It contains many items of interest connected with the tireless Methodist founder. In his lifetime, John Wesley rode a quarter of a million miles and preached more than forty-five thousand sermons in his mission to bring religion to the people.

JOHN WESLEY'S COTTAGE: The simple living room.

CARNIVAL TIME
Summer is incomplete without its village carnival and this photograph shows a group from the Altarnun carnival of 1961.

GYMKHANA
Sue Webb of Clemens Photography, Bodmin, spent a considerable time going through her late father's old photographs especially for this book. Here is a magnificent action shot taken at the Cardinham and Warleggan gymkhana of 1952 – Miss Moore and her grey clear a fence in impressive style.

BRITAIN IN BLOOM COMPETITION, about 1970
It may not look much now, but when summer comes the efforts of Phyllis Davey, Joyce Pooley, Pam Sandercock and Lionel Pooley will be rewarded with a riot of colour.

ALTARNUN CP SCHOOL, FIVE LANES
Although dwindling in numbers now, village schools have played a large part in the community life of moorland villages. Here with her pupils in the early 1960s is the teacher of Altarnun CP School, Pam Sandercock.

▼

ALTARNUN CELEBRATIONS
In 1959 this moorland village celebrated the centenary of its Methodist chapel. The minister on the right of the back row is the Rev Wilfred Wade, then Chairman of the Cornish Methodists.

ALTARNUN, 1951
Mr David Foot Nash is conducting a Wesley Day service beside the ford, before the building of a road bridge.

Seated on the parapet of the old bridge is Stanley Sowton, who was responsible for the restoration of Wesley's cottage at Trewint.

Car enthusiasts will no doubt recognise the classic lines of a Sunbeam Talbot in the foreground.

LAUNCESTON

Not strictly a moorland town, Launceston has always played an important part in the lives of moorland dwellers. It has provided them with market, inn, church – and gaol. This postcard, depicting St Thomas's Church in the background, was posted in Launceston in 1908, by T.N. Wenn and addressed to master P.W. Richards of Long Rock, Nr Penzance.

Launceston, St. Thomas' Church.

PEAT-CUTTERS

Working close to Brown Willy, these men would understand the tranquility of the moor in all its changing seasons. Peat-cutting was once a familiar sight on the peat bogs of the moor. Stacked and dried, peat provided fuel for the fires that warmed moorland cottages and cooked the food of isolated moorland residents.

Peatcutters, near Brown Willy

MARIKA HANBURY TENISON

Bodmin Moor has always attracted a great many men and
women who have shared their talents with the world. Writers,
poets, potters and artists among them. Travel and cookery
writer Marika Hanbury Tenison is seen here in the kitchen of
her moorland home. She died tragically early, in 1982.

ROUGH TOR

Workmen setting a plaque into position on the summit of
Rough Tor in the summer of 1954.

HELLAND CHURCH

 This lonely church, dedicated to Saint Helena was 'restored' almost beyond recognition at a time when JP St Aubyn was tearing the ancient heart out of so many churches in the area. Little is left of the old church, although there is an interesting old memorial to Humphrey Calwoodley and his wife who occupied the manor here in the 15th century.

PRINCE AND PRINCESS CHULA
Photographed in 1953 with Royal Navy Cadets at their
moorland home, Tredethy, Helland Bridge.
Before World War II, Prince Chula of Thailand owned a
number of racing cars which were driven with considerable
success by his cousin, Prince Bira. Both were well-known
figures at Brooklands. After the war, Prince Chula devoted his
time to writing, broadcasting, lecturing and making television
appearances.

TREDETHY, HELLAND BRIDGE
Now a country hotel, Tredethy can boast a superb view –
and a resident ghost. A butler from another century is said
occasionally to climb a staircase that is no longer in existence.
He no doubt feels very much at home in a house that boasts
wonderful log fires and a comfort that would appeal to the
head of any 'below stairs' establishment.

▶

*BLISLAND ANNUAL SHEEP
FAIR
During World War II
Cornwall played host to
many children evacuated
from the city to escape from
the bombing they had
suffered there.
I know from my own
wartime experience what a
traumatic time this was for
the children who might never
have seen a cow or a sheep.
Here, evacuee children
from Brentford and
Hackney, in London, are
seen getting to know the
animals at the sheep fair.*

HELLAND
    *Tredethy, home of Prince Chula was used as a sick bay to
house ill evacuees during the height of the blitz. Here staff are
seen with evacuees decorating a Christmas tree and preparing
to make a wartime Christmas as cheerful as rationing and
shortages would allow.*

BODMIN CHURCH SCHOOL
    *The infants at their
Christmas party in 1952 –
not many smiling faces but
perhaps the fun had not
really started.*

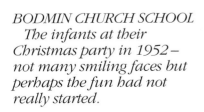

HELLAND BRIDGE

This is a very ancient bridge spanning the River Camel. Photographed by Ray Bishop in 1965, little has happened to change this quiet corner of Bodmin Moor.

◀

HELLAND CHAPEL

The inscription on the chapel tells the world that this is a Wesleyan Methodist Church, built in 1878. Cornwall's chapels, especially those on and about the moor, are as diverse and interesting as the men who built and preached in them. Some, like Isaac Foot, were men of great learning. Others, such as 'Foolish Dick' Hampton, were not. Yet all were joined in a faith which made them equals and helped moorland dwellers to look beyond the harshness of everyday moorland life.

PAUL JACKSON, MOORLAND POTTER

Paul Jackson moved to Cornwall in 1979, and established the Helland Pottery. He rapidly gained a reputation as one of Cornwall's foremost potters. Basing his ware initially on French and Italian ideas he later experimented with forms and decoration from all over the world. Eventually he developed a style that makes his pottery instantly recognisable as a Paul Jackson creation. In 1989 he relocated his pottery at Helland Bridge where he is here seen working.

PAUL JACKSON, MOORLAND POTTER

GILBERT MONUMENT, BODMIN
   The monument dominates Beacon Hill and overlooks Bodmin, the town from which the moor took its name. It was erected in memory of Sit Walter Raleigh Gilbert. A Cornishman, Sir Walter earned the grateful thanks of his country when he served as a Major General in the Sikh wars, during the mid-19th century.

CAMELFORD BRIDGE
   A tranquil scene that places this photograph somewhere about the turn of the century. It is difficult to imagine a moorland farmer attempting to drive his sheep across the bridge today. This town on the fringe of Bodmin Moor boasts the highest rainfall of any town in Cornwall.

Camelford Bridge.

ST BREWARD

Rubbing shoulders in St Breward are the church of St Breurdus and the Old Inn, dedicated to Bacchus. During the long history of the village, both have vied for the custom of the villagers.

SNOWFALL ON ROUGH TOR

For many moorland dwellers, this is one of the magic seasons of the year. Snow often falls here when the remainder of the county is snow-free. It brings with it an ageless silence that is a rarity at this end of the 20th century.

MUSEUM OF HISTORIC CYCLING, CAMELFORD

Earlier this century, many visitors to Bodmin Moor would have arrived by steam-train at Camelford Station – only to discover they had a long walk in order to reach the town which gave the station its name.

Perhaps some, wiser than their fellow-travellers, would have brought along a bicycle. If so, they would feel at home in the station today. A museum of cycling, it houses more than a hundred bicycles, among them this "Pollard" tandem tricycle of 1894. The tricycle is seen here ridden by the museum's proprietors, Sue and John Middleton.

CRADDOCK MOOR
Hardy moorland cattle graze near the Cheesewring Quarry. The famous balancing stones can just be seen on the skyline.

A SCENE NEAR BOWITHICK
This windswept slope, just off the Altarnun to Davidstow moorland road is typical of much of Bodmin Moor. Here are mossed, half-buried granite boulders and stunted wind-bowed trees paying homage to the prevailing wind. A visitor might be forgiven for imagining he is the first person ever to have come this way.

TEMPLE CHURCHYARD
This simple granite cross marks the grave of Charles Ernest Lambert. Rector of Warleggan and vicar of Temple. On the evening of Sunday, January 13, 1901, Lambert collapsed and died whilst walking across the moor to his Warleggan home after conducting evensong at Temple church. For three days and nights, until the body was discovered, his faithful Irish terrier remained at his dead master's side.
The occupants of Warleggan vicarage seemed prone to sad deaths. The last incumbent, the Reverend Frederick Densham, ostracised by his parishioners, died alone and lonely on the stairs of his rectory where he had lived the life of a recluse for some years.

BLISLAND CHURCH

The village of Blisland, with its traditional village green, is more reminiscent of England-across-the-Tamar than of Bodmin Moor. However, the church, dedicated to St Protus and St Hyacinth is one of the glories of the moor.

Sir John Betjeman once said: 'Of all the country churches of the West I have seen, I think the church of St Protus and Saint Hyacinth, Blisland, in Cornwall, is the most beautiful.'

In our 1952 photograph the Bluett and White families are joined in matrimony.

WEDDING OF RETURNED PoW

In common with the rest of Great Britain, Bodmin Moor saw many of its young men go off to war in 1939. Many became casualties, some were taken prisoner. Here is the wedding of a returned prisoner-of-war, George Partridge, who was married to Marjorie Guscott at Altarnun Church in 1945.

ITALIAN PRISON-OF-WAR, 1944
Many Italian prisoners-of-war worked on farms during the war and, as the war progressed they were given a great deal of freedom. Here, one PoW is seen working on Little Trehudreth Farm, Blisland.

◀

ST NEOT GYMKHANA

Horse shows and gymkhanas have long been popular summer events in Cornwall and nowhere more so than on Bodmin Moor.

These photographs were taken in 1952 by the late Clifford Clemens, of Bodmin. Clemens was a well-known press photograher whose work featured frequently in West Country newspapers.

It is possible that some readers may recognise the riders – or horses – featured here.

MOUNT CARNIVAL

A happy carnival queen and her attendants smile from their flower-decorated float in 1952's event.

73006. LISKEARD, PARADE AND WEBB'S HOTEL.

THE CHEESEWRING

THE PARADE.

LISKEARD

ST. CLEER WELL.

PARISH CHURCH.

WEBB'S HOTEL, LISKEARD

A photograph from a quieter, more relaxed age when 'traffic jams', 'yellow lines' and 'traffic wardens' had not yet entered the British vocabulary.

Liskeard was the arrival station for many who chose Bodmin Moor for their annual holiday destination. Webb's Hotel was an important and traditional venue for electioneering speeches, wedding receptions and the annual meetings and dinners for mines 'adventurers'.

LISKEARD

This 1917 postcard (postage charge a halfpenny, or a quarter of a 1992 penny!), shows four views of the Liskeard area.

The card was posted in Dobwalls and sent to an address in Dartmouth. It tells the addressee that 'Uncle Jack drove us to the Cheesewring' and implored 'Dot' to 'Look after Auntie Win and Grannie and help them to do the work'.

LANHYDROCK

71

LANHYDROCK

These parkland photographs of sheep and lambs were taken in the spring when the gardens of this splendid National Trust property are at their beautiful best.

Lanhydrock House, with its adjacent church, changed hands more than once during the Civil War of the 17th century and is today a popular venue for concerts featuring artists from all over the world.

NORTH CORNWALL HUNT
Seen here at Hamatethy, near St Breward in 1951 is the North Cornwall Hunt. Hunting, now a controversial issue, has had a considerable following on Bodmin Moor for many generations.

POLO TEAM
Although Prince Charles, the Duke of Cornwall, is a very keen polo player, it is not a game that is generally associated with Cornwall. This picture is, in fact, the Oxford University Polo team from earlier this century. Third from the left is a famous Cornishman, T.C. Agar-Robartes of Lanhydrock, one of the great Cornish houses and now a popular National Trust property.

Capt. T.C. Agar-Robartes was MP for Bodmin in 1906, and for St Austell 1908-1915. In the latter year, in the carnage of the French battlefields, he was recommended for the Victoria Cross after rescuing a wounded comrade under heavy enemy fire. Unfortunately, in September of the same year he died of wounds received in battle.

The Phœnix United Mines, Liskeard

From this vantage point the visitor has one of the finest views in all Cornwall – from Bodmin Moor, across the Tamar valley to Dartmoor on the far horizon.

The Phoenix mine has a fascinating, albeit a chequered history, but the Prince of Wales Shaft building must be one of the most photographed of all copper mine engine houses.

Moves are afoot to restore this building to its original glory and perhaps one day its walls may house a museum depicting the 19th century heyday of copper mining in East Cornwall.

MODERN DAY RIDERS

Modern farm buildings, but a very ancient moor. Bodmin Moor has seen every type of horseman and woman traversing its empty miles. Saxon Earles, Norman barons, Medieval knights, 18th century evangelists and 20th century pleasure seekers.

All have recognised the uniqueness of this moor which rises above the very heart of Cornwall.

It is here that I found inspiration for a number of my novels. Here too where Daphne du Maurier, on horseback and lost in a moorland mist, emerged to find – Jamaica Inn.

IDLE COTTAGE, SHARPTOR

Idle Cottage was the author's home on Bodmin Moor for many years. The cottage was known as 'The Idle Cottage' because it had lain idle for very many years after the closure of the Sharptor Mine not very far away. The slate slabs forming the path were once on the cottage floor. Removed some years before, the author laid the path on moving-in day, carrying down a slate slab and laying it in place after each trip to the cottage with an item of furniture.

From the door of the cottage there is a breathtaking view across the Tamar valley to Dartmoor, on the far horizon.

IDLE COTTAGE RESIDENTS, PAST AND PRESENT

Seen outside Idle Cottage are the author and son, Luke, together with the present occupants, Group Captain Paul Terrett, OBE and wife, Jean. They, like the author, saw and fell in love with the cottage, and have discovered for themselves the 'magic' of Bodmin Moor.

BODMIN AIRFIELD, CARDINHAM

Not yet up to Heathrow, or Kennedy Airport standards, the airfield at Cardinham is the headquarters of the Cornwall Flying Club and is very popular with Cornish fliers and well used by pilots of both gliders and powered aircraft.

CARDINHAM SHEEP MARKET, 1940
  The war was going badly for Great Britain and its allies. Talk
of invasion was in the air. But these old shepherds had seen it
all before. Boer War, World War I . . . Life had to go on,
Cardinham Sheep Market was at the heart of their everyday life. ▼

◀

ST BREWARD

Members of St Breward Band pose in front of Mr Clemen's camera for a presentation to the retiring bandmaster. St Breward Church is in the background. This photograph was taken in 1952. Forty years on the band continues to make music on the moor – and further afield.

THE TIMELESS MOOR

This photograph showing Brown Willy, Garrow Tor and Rough Tor was taken some fifty years ago. The scene it depicts might have looked exactly the same 100, 150 or even 200 years before.

Bodmin Moor is threatened as much by the late 20th century way of life as any other part of the country. Yet to come here and enjoy its ageless solitude is to return to a tranquility that helps to put the rest of the world into perspective.

This old wagon was once in use on a farm near St Breward, in the heart of the moor.

IMPLEMENTS FROM MOORLAND FARMS

Exhibits from the North Cornwall Museum and Gallery at Camelford, owned by Sally Holden and opened in 1974. The museum building was originally used for making coaches and wagons.

Here are two cloam ovens, used in Bodmin Moor farms and cottages for very many years. The oven on the left was manufactured at the well-known Lakes Pottery, in Truro. That on the right was an 'import', being made around 1820 by George Fishley of Fremington, North Devon. It was removed from the bakehouse at Lavethan Manor, Blisland.

WARLEGGAN WOOD
  Woodland areas are a rarity on Bodmin Moor. Most were cut down during mining days as fuel for engines, or cottage fires. This small area of woodland, near Warleggan seems to retain some of the mystery of the moor itself.

A Peat Knife. Peat from the bogs of Bodmin Moor was once of great importance to moorland dwellers, providing fuel for their cooking fires, heat for their homes and fertilisers for the thin soil of the moor.

NORTH CORNWALL MUSEUM

This is a bake iron (complete with pasty) used for baking in the ashes of an open fire. Irons such as this would have been a familiar sight in moorland kitchens.

WARLEGGAN CHURCH AND ANCIENT CROSS

This is one of the loneliest churches on Bodmin Moor. It is designed as though crouching against the ferocious blast of the winds that rage across the moor in winter. Once the church possessed a spire, but lightning claimed it in 1818.

The church's last resident rector was the sad and lonely Frederick Densham. Quarrelling with his parishioners, he was reduced to preaching his sermons to cut-out cardboard figures on a Sunday. During the week he lived the life of a recluse in his rectory.

When the war came and evacuee children were being trained out of London, the Reverend Densham made a playground in his garden for them and acquired a 'magic lantern' for their amusement. Unfortunately, he and his rectory were not considered to be a suitable place for young children and the playthings remained unused.

WARLEGGAN RIVER

Photographed as it passes through ancient woodland on its way from Bodmin moor, beneath Panters bridge to join up with another moorland river, the Fowey. (Many people think a more appropriate name for Bodmin Moor would be 'Fowey Moor').

CORNWALL'S OWN REGIMENT

Standing to attention on the parade ground of the now-empty Bodmin Barracks, are men of the Duke of Cornwall's Light Infantry.

The county has always been proud of its regiment. The memorials in Cornwall's towns and villages bear the names of some of the hundreds of Cornishmen who gave their lives on foreign battlefields whilst serving in its ranks.

The D.C.L.I. Museum in The Keep, at Bodmin provides a fascinating and moving record of the regiment and the men who proudly wore the uniforms on display. Here too are the eight Victoria Crosses awarded to the regiment, dating from the four awarded to those who took part in the desperate defence of Lucknow, to that won by Lt Phillip Curtis in 1953, during the Korean War.

WRNS, CORNISH STYLE

Given Cornwall's extensive coastline it is not surprising that the Women's Royal Naval Service should be stationed here. However, WRNS Rating Hall's place of duty was Glynn House, on the edge of Bodmin Moor – some distance from the sea!

MILITARY POLICEMAN, US ARMY STYLE

During World War II many United States servicemen were stationed in Cornwall. Private Bencekovich was a military policeman stationed in Bodmin Barracks and he would have had a busy time. American and British servicemen were allies in battle but they did not always hold the same views when they met up after an evening spent drinking.

DCLI BAND, MARCHING THROUGH BODMIN
A regimental band marching through a town has always
been calculated to draw young men to enlist. Perhaps this was
the intention of the band of Cornwall's own regiment,
marching through the county town in wartime.

ALTARNUN HOME GUARD

Every community in Great Britain had its own 'Dad's Army'. Mustered at a time when invasion from across the English Channel was a real threat, they were prepared to 'give their all' for their country. On Bodmin Moor their greatest danger was probably of becoming lost during night exercises. This photograph dates from 1944 when some Home Guard units were already being disbanded.

BATHING BEAUTIES, 1942

One of the more pleasant duties of a wartime Chief Constable must have been presenting prizes to the winners of beauty competitions.

Major 'Bunny' Hare, who was also president of 'Aid to Russia', is seen here with the prizewinners of the senior and junior beauty competitions, held at Bodmin.

HM KING GEORGE VI AT LISKEARD
   On May 7, 1942, His Majesty King George VI arrived at the
Great Western Railway station at Liskeard, accompanied by
Queen Elizabeth for a tour of the area. Here they are seen
being greeted by local dignitaries.

ACCIDENT ON BODMIN MOOR

Sadly, this is a far more familiar sight today than it was in 1945 when this photograph was taken. Vehicles were also considerably slower. (Just as well in view of the absence of all tread on the front nearside tyre!)

The accident claimed a victim in the form of a cow which wandered on the road in front of the lorry. In those days of rationing the accident no doubt provided an unexpected bonus for a great many families.

AIR RAID ON BODMIN, 1942

Bodmin received a visit from the German Luftwaffe on August 7, 1942. In this photograph the army is seen helping a Rescue Squad clear wreckage from a bombed house in which eleven people were trapped.

THE STANNON CIRCLE

Another evocative drawing by Felicity Young of Tintagel. The Stannon Circle stands on the western edge of Bodmin Moor, in St Breward Parish. This stone circle contains more than seventy stones, most small and irregularly spaced.

MORE BOSSINEY BOOKS . . .

DISCOVERING BODMIN MOOR

by E.V. Thompson, 45 photographs and map.
E.V. Thompson, author of the bestselling novel, *Chase the Wind,* set on the eastern slopes of Bodmin Moor, explores the Moor past and present.
'. . . shows the moor in all its aspects – beautiful, harsh, romantic and almost cruel . . . how well he knows the character of the moor.'
The Editor, Cornish Guardian

E.V. THOMPSON'S WESTCOUNTRY

This is a memorable journey: a combination of colour and black-and-white photography. Bristol to Land's End happens to be the Bossiney region, and this is precisely E.V. Thompson's Westcountry.
'Stunning photographs and fascinating facts make this an ideal book for South West tourists and residents alike . . .'
Jane Leigh, Express & Echo

DAPHNE DU MAURIER COUNTRY

by Martyn Shallcross
A very special look at Cornwall in that the internationally-famous novelist has set important stories here. Explores locations which fired Dame Daphne's imagination. The subject of a Radio Cornwall series, produced by Tamsin Thomas.
'. . . Anyone whose appreciation of the beauty of Cornwall has been enhanced by Dame Daphne's writing will enjoy this book – a fitting tribute to a remarkable lady.'
Cornish Life

MY CORNWALL

A personal vision of Cornwall by eleven writers who lived and worked in the county: Daphne du Maurier, Ronald Duncan, James Turner, Angela du Maurier, Jack Clemo, Denys Val Baker, Colin Wilson, C.C. Vyvyan, Arthur Caddick, Michael Williams and Derek Tangye with reproductions of paintings by Margo Maeckelberghe.
'An ambitious collection of chapters.'
The Times, London

FOWEY – RIVER AND TOWN

by Sarah Foot
An enlarged and updated edition of Following the River Fowey.
'The intricate tapestries of this delightful area are woven together with warm, understanding interviews . . . buy, beg or borrow it.'
The Cornish Times

KING ARTHUR COUNTRY in CORNWALL, THE SEARCH for the REAL ARTHUR

by Brenda Duxbury, Michael WIlliams and Colin Wilson
Over 50 photographs and 3 maps
An exciting exploration of the Arthurian sites in Cornwall and Scilly, including the related legends of Tristan and Iseult, with The Search for the Real Arthur by Colin Wilson.
'. . . provides a refreshing slant on an old story linking it with the present.'
Caroline Righton, The Packet Newspapers

MYSTERIES IN THE CORNISH LANDSCAPE

by Tamsin Thomas of Radio Cornwall
A tour of thirty historic locations in Cornwall by the well-known Cornish broadcaster, starting at Chun Castle down in the Hundred of Penwith and ending at The Hurlers on the eastern edge of Bodmin Moor.
'Tamsin takes us on an enjoyable and speculative canter – literally for she is often on horseback – through these fascinating and often controversial features of old Kernow.'
Donald Rawe, Cornish Scene
'Tamsin has produced a delightful book which will enchant her audience.'
Ronnie Hoyle, The Western Morning News

AROUND & ABOUT THE SMUGGLERS' WAYS

by David Mudd
Working through almost forty different sources, including the records of H.M. Customs & Excise itself, David Mudd (who discovered in the course of his research that his great-grandfather was a Customs officer) has produced a book that is as heady and addictive as the spirits, the wines and the tobaccos that once followed fish, tin and copper as Cornwall's great industries. Several of the sketches and many of the photographs are by David's wife, Diana.
'. . . scrapes the romantic glitter from Cornwall's erstwhile illicit trade . . . Meticulously researched and written in David Mudd's lively factual style it makes absorbing reading.'
Alison Poole, Leader Group of Newspapers

GHOSTS OF CORNWALL

by Peter Underwood
Peter Underwood, President of the Ghost Club, journeys across haunted Cornwall. Photographs of haunted sites and drawings of ghostly characters all combine to prove that Cornwall is indeed a mystic land.

MORE BOSSINEY BOOKS . . .

WEST CORNWALL CAMERA
Photographs: Harry Penhaul
Text: Douglas Williams

MOUNT'S BAY
by Douglas Williams

LEGENDS OF CORNWALL
by Sally Jones

**PARANORMAL IN THE
WESTCOUNTRY**
by Michael Williams

**SUPERNATURAL SEARCH IN
CORNWALL**
by Michael Williams

EAST CORNWALL IN THE OLD DAYS
by Joy Wilson

**OLD PICTURE POST CARDS OF
CORNWALL**
by Sara Paston-Williams

STRANGE STORIES OF CORNWALL
by David & Diana Mudd, John Hocking, Joy Wilson,
Felicity Young & Michael Williams

ABOUT LAND'S END
by Wendy Lewis

CASTLES OF CORNWALL
by Mary & Hal Price

THE RIVER TAMAR
by Sarah Foot

We shall be pleased to send you our catalogue giving
full details of our growing list of titles for Devon,
Cornwall, Dorset, Somerset and Wiltshire and forth-
coming publications. If you have difficulty in obtain-
ing our titles, write direct to Bossiney Books, Land's
End, St Teath, Bodmin, Cornwall.